I0520571

FAITH UNDER FIRE

A 30-Day Devotional for First Responders

FAITH UNDER FIRE

— A 30-Day Devotional for First Responders —

Erick Hurt

**GOSPEL
SUPPORT**
PUBLISHING

© 2025 Erick Hurt
All rights reserved.

No part of this book may be reproduced, stored in a retrieval system, or transmitted in any form or by any means without prior written permission from the author, except in the case of brief quotations used in articles or reviews.

Scripture quotations taken from The Holy Bible, New International Version®, NIV®. Copyright © 1973, 1978, 1984, 2011 by Biblica, Inc. Used with permission of Zondervan. All rights reserved worldwide. www.zondervan.com

Scripture quotations marked (NLT) are taken from the Holy Bible, New Living Translation, copyright ©1996, 2004, 2015 by Tyndale House Foundation. Used by permission of Tyndale House Publishers, Carol Stream, Illinois 60188. All rights reserved.

Unless otherwise indicated, all Scripture quotations are from The ESV® Bible (The Holy Bible, English Standard Version®), © 2001 by Crossway, a publishing ministry of Good News Publishers. Used by permission. All rights reserved.

Why One Devotional a Day?

This devotional was intentionally designed to be read one lesson per day. Not because the content is long, but because the goal is depth. True spiritual transformation doesn't come through quickly consuming truths but through slowing down and allowing the Holy Spirit to do His work in the heart.

Each day's reading is meant to be meditated on, prayed through, and lived out. Reflection questions are included not to fill time, but to create space for meditation, clarity, and response. When we rush past truth, we often miss its transforming power. When we slow down, the Lord has room to reveal, renew, and refine.

This pace also gives opportunity to grow in self-control, one of the beautiful fruits of the Spirit (Galatians 5:22–23). Holding back the urge to move ahead—even when it's "just one more"—shows the maturity and growth needed to lead others in Christ. So resist the urge to hurry. Take your time. And let each day's lesson linger.

Using This Devotional in a Group Setting

This 30-day devotional was designed not only for personal growth, but also to support group study and discussion. If you're going through this with a small group, Bible study, or church class, you'll find a simple **Leader's Guide** at the back of this book.

The Leader's Guide includes:

- A suggested weekly group format
- Discussion prompts for each devotional
- Application questions to help your group reflect and respond
- Space for additional notes and insights

Whether you're leading two people or twenty, this guide will help you keep the focus on Christ and make space for real connection and transformation.

Table of Contents

Introduction

Faith Under Fire: A 30-Day Devotional for First Responders

Every firefighter knows what it means to face the flames—but not every fire burns outside the walls. Some fires rage quietly within: stress, anger, guilt, fear, or the weight of what you've seen and carried. The uniform may hide it, but the heart still feels it.

This devotional was written for those who run toward danger and serve in the heat of battle—both physically and spiritually. Whether you're on the fireground, behind the badge, or standing beside someone who is, *Faith Under Fire* will help you find peace, purpose, and identity in Jesus Christ.

Because while the fire tests your strength, faith reveals your foundation.

Over the next 30 days, you'll discover how the gospel meets you right where you are—in the middle of real pressure, real pain, and real purpose. You'll see that faith isn't about pretending to be strong; it's about trusting the One who is. Jesus didn't promise a life without fire, but He did promise to be with you in it—and to bring you through it refined, not destroyed.

Each day includes:

- A title to center your focus
- A Scripture passage to anchor your soul
- A short devotional to strengthen your faith
- A prayer to steady your heart
- Reflection questions to apply what you've learned

This journey isn't about trying to be tougher, stronger, or better. It's about learning to stand firm when life gets hot—to trust the God who walks with you through every flame.

Take it one day at a time. Let the truth of God's Word quench your fear, renew your mind, and reignite your hope. You may wear the gear, but God supplies the grace.

No matter what fire you face, you are never alone.

Day 1 – First In, Last Out

Truth for Today: John 15:13

"Greater love has no one than this, that someone lay down his life for his friends."

This is what we signed up for. We knew the risks and the weight of the badge. We said yes to being the ones who run in when others look on—not for fame, but for the people, the brotherhood, and the community. For those who need help when their world is on fire.

There's something sacred about that kind of sacrifice—and that's why Jesus' words hit home: *"Greater love has no one than this, that someone lay down his life for his friends."* And it's not just for friends—it's for strangers too. We willingly put ourselves in harm's way for people we may never meet again. That's the calling. That's the gospel.

Jesus didn't just talk about sacrifice—He lived it, and gave His life on the cross, laying it down for the world. He paid the ultimate price to rescue us, not from physical flames, but from the fire of God's judgment, sin, and death. He didn't hesitate, running into the fire with you on His mind—with you in His heart.

He is the ultimate First Responder. He went in first and came out victorious—making a way for you to be saved, healed, and brought into the family of God. His mission was to rescue, redeem, and restore–you. And He set the example for every firefighter, paramedic, EMT and officer who's ever laid it all on the line for someone else.

This is the love that changes everything. The love that fuels our sacrifice. The love that went before us and makes every risk worth it. You were the one He came to rescue. You are the one He still loves.

Let His example define your purpose—not just as a first responder, but as a man or woman who gives their life away. First in, last out—like Jesus did for you.

Prayer

Lord, thank You for going first—for running into the fire of judgment so I could be saved. Help me to follow Your example in courage, love, and sacrifice. Remind me daily that You laid down Your life for me, and give me the strength to lay mine down for others.

Reflection Questions

1. How does Jesus' sacrifice give new meaning to the risks you take on the job?

_____

_____

_____

_____

_____

2. In what ways can you reflect Christ's love to those you serve—both on and off duty?

_____

_____

_____

_____

_____

3. Have you personally received the rescue Jesus offers?

_____

_____

_____

_____

_____

_____

_____

_____

_____

_____

_____

_____

Day 2 – When the Alarm Sounds

Truth for Today: Isaiah 6:8

"Then I heard the voice of the Lord saying, 'Whom shall I send? And who will go for us?' And I said, 'Here am I. Send me!'"

---

*E*very time the alarm sounds, something stirs inside—a jolt of adrenaline, a surge of anticipation, a hint of uneasiness. It doesn't matter if you just started your shift, sat down for a hot meal, or were deep in sleep—when the bell rings, you answer the call.

We signed up knowing this reality, but no training could prepare us for the toll it would take over time. The interrupted sleep. The stress on our minds and bodies. The emotional weight. Still, we go—not for recognition or reward, but because deep down we want to help others. We were made to respond. It's a calling.

And that calling mirrors the heart of Christ.

In Isaiah 6, when the Lord asks, "Whom shall I send?—the prophet responds, "Here am I. Send me!" That willingness to step in, to go where others won't, points us to Christ Himself. When the alarm sounded in heaven, Jesus answered, "Here I am, send Me." He left His place in paradise, stepped into our broken world, and came to rescue us—not from a burning building, but from sin and death—eternal separation from God.

Romans says: "But God demonstrates his own love for us in this: While we were still sinners, Christ died for us." (Romans 5:8). Jesus didn't come to be served, but to serve—out of love for you. Willingly and fully knowing the cost.

That same heart beats in every firefighter and first responder who says yes when the world says run. The alarm calls us to more than action—it calls us to sacrifice, to service, and sometimes to suffering.

But when we know who went before us, who gave everything to rescue us, we find strength to keep answering that call. Every time the bell rings, remember this; your courage, your strength, and your response are meeting someone else's greatest need.

Prayer

Lord, thank You for answering the call when I couldn't. You stepped down from heaven and entered the fire for my sake. Give me a heart like Yours—ready, willing, and full of love. When the alarm sounds, help me to respond not just with action, but with faith and trust in You.

Reflection Questions

1. When have you felt God calling you to act—not just on duty, but in life?

_____

_____

_____

_____

_____

2. How does Jesus' willingness to leave heaven inspire your own service?

_____

_____

_____

_____

_____

3. What might it look like today to say, "Here am I. Send me"?

_____

_____

_____

_____

_____

_____

_____

_____

_____

_____

_____

_____

Day 3 – Through the Fire

Truth for Today: Isaiah 43:2

"When you walk through the fire, you shall not be burned, and the flame shall not consume you."

---

*B*eing a first responder can feel lonely—even faithless at times. We carry more than the physical weight of gear. We carry the weight of what we've seen, what we've lost, and what we can't unsee. The calls don't stop. The pressure doesn't ease. The expectation to be strong never wavers.

And yet, deep down, many feel like they're walking through the fire alone.

Some bury the pain—hiding it under layers of toughness or silence. Others try to cope through outlets that only create more damage. Still others quietly burn out, retiring early or quitting altogether—not because they stopped caring, but because the fire inside became an inferno.

Isaiah 43:2 doesn't say if you walk through the fire—it says when. Crisis is a guarantee, but so is God's power and presence. He promises, "When you walk through the fire, you shall not be burned… the flame shall not consume you." That's not just wishful thinking—it's a promise.

God is with you on the call, in the madness, and in the silence afterward. He walks into crisis with you. He never leaves you. Never abandons you. Never forgets you.

Jesus knows exactly what it feels like to walk through fire. He came to earth wrapped in frail humanity, taking on our pain, our stress, our fear, and our sin.

And on the cross, He walked through the ultimate fire—the fire of God's judgment—alone. He bore the full weight of sin and suffering, so that we could walk through our own fires with Him by our side.

He understands. He cares. He is with you—in the heat, in the heartbreak, and in the healing.

So when the pressure builds, when you feel like no one understands, when you're on your last ounce of strength—lean into the One who walked through the fire for you, and walks through the fire with you.

Prayer

Lord, You know the weight I carry. You've walked through the fire before me. Thank You for never leaving me alone in the crisis. Help me to sense Your presence even in the heat of battle, and to lean on You when my strength runs out. You are my refuge, my peace, and my hope.

Reflection Questions

1. What pressures or pain are you walking through right now?

_____

_____

_____

_____

_____

2. How does knowing Jesus has walked through fire encourage you in your role as a first responder?

_____

_____

_____

_____

_____

3. What would it look like for you to lean on Jesus more intentionally today?

_____

_____

_____

_____

_____

_____

_____

_____

_____

_____

_____

_____

Day 4 – Standing in the Gap

Truth for Today: Ezekiel 22:30

"I looked for someone among them who would build up the wall and stand before me in the gap on behalf of the land..."

---

*A*s a first responder, you're always standing in the gap, between danger and disaster, between crisis and chaos. Whether it's an emergency call, a structure fire, a medical response, or simply being a steady presence at home, you're often the one holding the line when everything else is falling apart.

A call comes in for a heart attack—and you're the one standing in the gap for that family.

A call comes in for a fire—and you're there between the flames and the people who can't save themselves.

It's more than a job. It's a calling, not just a career. You're the provider, the protector, the one who shows up when someone's world is unraveling. But you're not alone in that role.

Jesus stood in the gap in the most powerful way imaginable. On the cross, He hung between two criminals—between heaven and earth—bridging the gap between sinful humanity and a holy God. He laid His life down to save ours. He is the One who stepped into the fire of judgment to pull us out.

Not only did He die in our place, but He lives now to intercede for us—praying, protecting, guiding. He sent His Spirit to comfort, counsel, to strengthen us when our strength runs out, to live in us forever—and to guide us into all truth.

Because Jesus stood in the gap for you, you now stand in the gap for others—not just physically, but spiritually. You're not just a first responder; you're a lifeline—an encourager, a friend to the grieving, a light in the darkness, a comforting voice when the world is spinning out of control.

And just like Jesus is always present, you're called to reflect that presence in the lives you touch—whether they notice or not. Whether they thank you or not.

You may be the only glimpse of love and hope some people ever see—you matter more than you know—and your presence alone may have silently saved a life.

Prayer

Jesus, thank You for standing in the gap for me—for bridging the distance between my sin and God's holiness. Help me reflect Your love as I serve others. When I respond to the call, let me carry not just skill, but compassion. Teach me to pray, to comfort, and to stand strong in the Spirit for those who are hurting.

Reflection Questions

1. Where in your life are you currently standing in the gap for someone?

_____

_____

_____

_____

_____

2. How does Jesus' sacrifice help you stay grounded when the pressure is building?

_____

_____

_____

_____

_____

3. Who around you needs more than just physical help—who needs prayer, compassion, or a word of hope?

_____

_____

_____

_____

_____

_____

_____

_____

_____

_____

_____

_____

_____

Day 5 – The Weight of the Gear

Truth for Today: Hebrews 12:1

"Let us throw off everything that hinders and the sin that so easily entangles. And let us run with endurance the race marked out for us."

$\mathcal{W}$hether it's gearing up for a fire, loading a patient onto the gurney, or carrying the trauma bag like a backpack, the weight adds up. The gear is heavy, and the calls are even heavier. Over time, the burden takes a toll—not just on the body, but on the heart and mind as well.

Being a first responder demands endurance. You literally have to stay in shape—physically, mentally, emotionally, and spiritually—to run the race of this career. But the gear isn't the only weight we carry. There's the silent burden of trauma, the emotional cost of loss, and the pressure to always be strong.

And yet, even this weight points us to something greater. Hebrews 12:1 reminds us to throw off everything that hinders and to run with endurance the race before us. It doesn't say the weight isn't real—it says don't let it entangle you. Why? Because Jesus bore the real burden.

On the cross, Jesus took on the full weight of our sin—a burden far heavier than turnout gear, trauma bag, or years of stress combined. He carried the crushing load of guilt, shame, judgment, and death. And He did it for you. He endured the cross, scorning its shame, finished the mission, and rose with power over death.

Talk about strength! Talk about endurance!

So when your gear feels too heavy, when the burden of the job seems too much, fix your eyes on Him—the One who carried the cross, who carried your sins, and who gives you strength to endure whatever you face. He doesn't just understand your load—He carried His own to free you from yours.

Let Jesus be your example and your sustainer. Lean on Him. Look to Him. Trust in Him. He will help you throw off every weight and give you the endurance to finish your race. You're not running this race alone—He's been running it with you the whole time.

Prayer

Lord, You carried the heaviest burden—my sin, my shame, my guilt—and You did it out of love for me. Help me to lay down every weight that's slowing me down. Strengthen me to endure the race You've set before me. When the job is overwhelming, remind me to fix my eyes on You—the One who finished it all.

Reflection Questions

1. What burdens are you carrying right now—physically, mentally, or spiritually?

_____

_____

_____

_____

2. How does knowing Jesus bore the weight of your sin help you in seasons of weariness?

_____

_____

_____

_____

3. What can you "throw off" today to run your race with more freedom?

_____

_____

_____

_____

_____

_____

_____

_____

_____

_____

_____

_____

Day 6 - The Thin Red Line

Truth for Today: Psalm 144:1

"Praise be to the Lord my Rock, who trains my hands for war, my fingers for battle."

---

*W*hen we signed up to be a first responder, we didn't think of it as training for battle. We just wanted to help people—to be the one who was there in a time of need when others stood back and watched. If someone needed to be pulled from a fire, bandaged up, or rescued from a crisis, we wanted to be there as part of that team. Part of the solution.

But over time, we discovered this life is a battle—not just physically, but emotionally and spiritually. The alarms keep ringing. The calls replay in your mind when you're tossing and turning. You run on caffeine, soda, half-eaten meals, and a whole lot of heart. Through it all, your hands are being trained—not just in skills, but in sacrifice.

And you don't walk through this alone. You're part of a team that fights side by side—bound by courage, a common mission, and shared suffering. You're in it for each other, and for the ones you serve.

Jesus knows that kind of battle. He stepped into a world of people in need of rescue. He is the One who trained for battle with a cross on His back and nails in His hands. He hung on His own thin red line—the blood running from His wounds in His hands and feet to the ground below—as He fought for your life. He didn't run from the fire of God's judgment. He ran into it willingly—for you.

So when your hands grow tired, or you're weary from the calls, look to the life He gave you. And when the alarm sounds, remember the battle He already won for you. He hung in your place so you could stand in His strength.

Prayer

Lord, my hands grow tired. The burden feels heavy. But I thank You that You went to battle for me. Help me to draw strength from Your sacrifice and remember that I never fight alone.

Reflection Questions

1. What "battle" are you feeling most right now —
   emotional, physical, or spiritual?

   _____

   _____

   _____

   _____

2. Have you handed that over to the One who
   already won the war for you?

   _____

   _____

   _____

   _____

3. How can you let Christ's example of sacrifice and courage shape the way you serve and support those on your team today?

_____

_____

_____

_____

_____

_____

_____

_____

_____

_____

_____

_____

Day 7 – On the Front Lines

Truth for Today: Ephesians 6:10–11

"Finally, be strong in the Lord and in his mighty power. Put on the full armor of God, so that you can take your stand against the devil's schemes."

---

*A*s first responders, we're always on the front lines. We suit up, check our gear, and prepare for the unknown—because lives are on the line. But while we train for physical danger, there's another kind of battle we face every day. One that doesn't sound an alarm or flash with red lights. One that hits deeper—internally.

- It's the battle within.
- For your peace.
- For your purpose.

Spiritual warfare is just as real as any structure fire or medical call. It shows up in the form of fear, shame, isolation, temptation, and the haunting memories that creep in after the call is over. That's why the Bible tells us not to face this fight alone or unarmed—but to put on the full armor of God.

This armor is more than metaphor; it's a daily necessity:

- The helmet of salvation protects your mind. You're not defined by your failures or your past, but by your identity in Christ—saved, loved, and secure. The helmet helps clear the clutter in your thoughts.

- The breastplate of righteousness protects your heart. You've been made new. No longer condemned, but forgiven and given a new heart.

- The shield of faith stops the fiery arrows of the enemy—those subtle lies that say, "You're not enough. You've failed again. You're all alone."

- The belt of truth holds it all together. It keeps you grounded in God's promises when everything around you is unstable. Jesus is the truth that sets you free!

- The sword of the Spirit—God's Word—is your weapon, by which you are able to stand firm.

You would never run into a burning building without your turnout gear. So why step into a spiritual battlefield without your armor?

The truth is, you're not fighting for victory—you're fighting from it. Jesus already won the war on the cross, and the proof was in His resurrection. Now He invites you to stand firm in His finished work.

So the next time you wake up to the weight of the day—or the next call shakes your spirit—remember; you're not just a first responder—you're on the front lines of spiritual warfare. So gear up!

Prayer

Lord, help me to recognize the spiritual battles I face and not to fight in my own strength. Thank You that You've already won the war through the cross. Teach me to daily put on Your armor, to stand firm in truth, and to go forward with courage. Be my strength on the front lines.

Reflection Questions

1. Which piece of God's armor do you most often overlook?

_____

_____

_____

_____

2. How can you practically "put on" the armor each morning?

_____

_____

_____

_____

_____

3. Where are you currently feeling pressure or spiritual attack?

_____

_____

_____

_____

_____

_____

_____

_____

_____

_____

Day 8 – Faith Under Fire

Truth for Today: 1 Peter 1:6–7

"In this you greatly rejoice, though now for a little while you may have had to suffer grief in all kinds of trials. These have come so that the proven genuineness of your faith—of greater worth than gold, which perishes even though refined by fire—may result in praise, glory and honor when Jesus Christ is revealed."

$\mathcal{F}$ire tests everything. It reveals what is solid and what will melt away. On the job, we know that structures can look stable until the heat exposes their weakness. The same can be true for our faith. It may look strong on the outside, but trials have a way of proving what we're really built on.

As first responders, we walk into literal fires—risking our lives to save others. But many of us are also walking through personal fires: family stress, trauma, grief, addictions, burnout, depression. We don't always talk about it, but we carry it with us, and it smolders beneath the surface.

Peter's words remind us that our trials are not meaningless. They are a refining fire. Not punishment—but a process. God isn't trying to destroy you in the fire; He's shaping and strengthening you. Just as gold is refined in the heat, your faith is being purified in the pressures you face. He is after something eternal in you—something that will last long after the firehouse, and even after this life has passed.

Jesus walked into a literal fire of death for us. He was tested in every way and came through pure, spotless, and faithful. He now walks with us through our own flames. Not from a distance, but right in the middle of it. He knows your thoughts, your fears, your struggles—and He's not ashamed of you. He is refining you.

So don't be discouraged if you feel like your faith is being stretched thin. Maybe that's the very place God is strengthening it. Let the fire reveal Christ in you. Let it burn off the weight you weren't meant to carry. And when it's all said and done, may your faith bring glory and honor to Christ—the One who stood in the fire with you.

Prayer

Lord, I feel the heat of the fire in my life—at work, at home, and in my heart. Sometimes I want to quit or run, but I trust that You are using this fire to refine me, not ruin me. Strengthen my faith. Burn off anything in me that's not from You. And help me walk through the flames with courage, knowing You are always with me.

Reflection Questions

1. What trial or "fire" are you walking through right now?

_____

_____

_____

_____

2. How might God be using it to refine your faith rather than destroy it?

_____

_____

_____

_____

3. What's one burden you can give to God today instead of carrying it alone?

_____

_____

_____

_____

_____

_____

_____

_____

_____

_____

_____

_____

_____

Day 9 – Answering the Call

Truth for Today: Romans 12:1

"Therefore, I urge you, brothers and sisters, in view of God's mercy, to offer your bodies as a living sacrifice, holy and pleasing to God—this is your true and proper worship."

---

*E*very time the tones drop, you answer the call. Whether it's a car wreck, a medical call, or a structure fire—you respond without hesitation. That's what you're here for. You've trained for it. You've trained your life for this sacrifice. But behind every shift, every sleepless night, and every rescue, there's something deeper happening; you're offering your life in service to others.

Paul writes in Romans that the way we truly worship God is by offering our bodies—our very lives—as living sacrifices. This isn't just about our work; it's about our why. When you answer the call with integrity, courage, and compassion, you're doing more than fulfilling a job description—you're living out a spiritual calling to serve.

That's the difference between duty and devotion. And before you ever responded to your first emergency, Jesus responded to your greatest need. Jesus answered the call to leave heaven, take on flesh, and lay down His life for you.

You may not feel like what you do is worship, but every moment you lay down your rights, your comfort, and your time for the sake of someone else—you're worshiping. You're honoring God by reflecting the heart of Christ, who came not to be served but to serve and to give His life as a ransom for many.

Your purpose isn't just found in your position. Your purpose is found in the One who called you to love sacrificially, and to walk faithfully with Him. That's what makes your sacrifice "holy and pleasing to God."

So as you gear up for another call, and know this; your life of service matters to God. He sees every act of courage, every quiet moment of compassion, and every sacrifice you make. Keep offering it all to Him—and let that be your greatest act of worship.

Prayer

Lord, I want to live a life of purpose. Help me offer every part of who I am to You—my time, my body, my mind, and my heart. Thank You for answering the call to rescue me. May I live in a way that honors You, even in the unseen moments of sacrifice.

Reflection Questions

1. What does it mean for you to live as a "living sacrifice" in your role?

_____

_____

_____

_____

2. Are there areas of your life you need to give more fully to God?

_____

_____

_____

_____

3. How does Jesus' ultimate sacrifice inspire your daily service?

_____

_____

_____

_____

_____

_____

_____

_____

_____

_____

_____

_____

Day 10 – Hydrated and Ready

Truth for Today: John 4:14

"But whoever drinks the water I give them will never thirst. Indeed, the water I give them will become in them a spring of water welling up to eternal life."

---

*Y*ou don't need to be told how important hydration is on the job. Whether it's a structure fire, a medical emergency, or an extended rescue, staying hydrated isn't optional—it's critical. Dehydration leads to fatigue, confusion, and even collapse. You train for this, plan for it, and keep the water close at hand.

But how often do we forget about spiritual dehydration? You can have all the physical gear, training, and strength, but without being spiritually refreshed, you'll dry up inside—drained by the demands of the job, the brokenness you witness, and the burdens you carry.

In John 4, Jesus tells the woman at the well that He offers a kind of water this world can't provide. Not bottled or filtered—but living water—His Spirit poured into those who believe. It's not a one-time drink; it becomes a spring inside you constantly flowing, constantly renewing, and never running dry.

Maybe you've been running on fumes lately. The weight of what you've seen, the grief of loss, the relentless schedule—it's enough to wear anyone down. Jesus offers more than momentary relief. He thirsted on that cross so you would never have to thirst again. He was poured out so you could be filled. Because He died and rose again, His Spirit now lives in you as an endless well of hope, strength, peace, and renewal.

When you drink deeply from Christ—by believing in Him—you'll find He quenches your soul in ways nothing else can. And when you're filled with His living water, you're not only refreshed, you become a source of refreshment for others.

So yes, hydrate your body, and keep the bottle nearby, but don't neglect your soul. Make time to sit at the well with Jesus. He's already there, waiting. He knows you're tired and weary. He hears your silent prayers. And He knows exactly what you need to keep going.

Prayer

Jesus, I need Your living water today. I'm tired, dry, and often overwhelmed. Fill me with Your Spirit. Quench the thirst of my soul. Let Your presence renew me and make me a spring of refreshment to others.

Reflection Questions

1. Have you been trying to serve others while spiritually dehydrated?

_____

_____

_____

_____

_____

2. What are some ways you can intentionally drink from Christ's living water each day?

_____

_____

_____

_____

_____

3. Who in your life needs you to be a source of
    spiritual refreshment?

_____

_____

_____

_____

_____

_____

_____

_____

_____

_____

_____

_____

Day 11 – 24 Hour Trust

Truth for Today: Psalm 121:4

"Indeed, he who watches over Israel will neither slumber nor sleep."

---

*S*ome of the hardest moments in a first responder's life happen in the middle of the night. The city sleeps, but you're always ready for the next call. Darkness settles, and silence is often pierced by sirens or cries for help. Whether you're at the station, or driving into unknown scenes, the shift tests more than your strength—it tests your trust.

Psalm 121 is a reminder that while the world sleeps, God doesn't. He never drifts off, gets distracted, or takes breaks. He is always watching, always present, and always able. You may feel alone in the early hours of the morning, but you are never alone—or unprotected. The God who called the stars by name is still watching over you—on every call, every minute, of every moment.

And this promise isn't built on hope alone. It's grounded in the gospel. Because Jesus went to the cross and rose again, you are no longer alone in your struggles—you are united with Him. The One who never sleeps is the same One who once slept in a storm-tossed boat—fully human—yet rose from the grave in full authority over death.

He didn't just promise peace—He purchased it with His blood. And now, by grace through faith, you belong to Him.

Trusting God in the dark isn't just about being brave—it's about being anchored in Christ. It's the quiet confidence that comes from knowing His eyes never close, His care never wavers, and His love has already been proven through His death. The psalmist doesn't just say God is awake—he says God is watching over you. That's personal, intimate, and what Jesus came to accomplish.

Only Jesus can guard your soul when you're exhausted, your body when you're vulnerable, and your mind when it starts to drift. When you're tired, remember He never tires. When you can't see, remember He is your guiding Light. And when fear creeps in, remember the One who gave His life for yours is still on watch—you're under the ever-watchful eyes of your Savior.

Prayer

Father, thank You that You never slumber. And because of Jesus, I can rest in more than just safety—I can rest in salvation. While I sleep, or while I work through the night, remind me that I'm never alone. Teach me to trust You in the dark, to find peace in Your presence, and to remember the cross every time I need reassurance.

Reflection Questions

1. What fears or anxieties tend to rise during your shift or in the dark?

_____

_____

_____

_____

2. How does the gospel help you trust God's care—not just emotionally, but literally and eternally?

_____

_____

_____

_____

3. What would it look like to rest in Christ's finished work tonight?

_____

_____

_____

_____

_____

_____

_____

_____

_____

_____

_____

_____

Day 12 – Every Second Counts

Truth for Today: James 4:14

"What is your life? You are a mist that appears for a little while and then vanishes."

$\mathcal{N}$o one understands urgency like a first responder. When the tones sound, there's no time to waste. Every second counts. Heartbeats, shallow breaths, flames, and fading consciousness don't wait for convenience—they demand a response. You've likely witnessed moments where just a few seconds made the difference between life and death.

James reminds us of something we often ignore in the rush of life; that our time here on earth is short. We are a mist—a vapor that appears for a moment, then vanishes. That's not meant to scare or discourage, but to awaken us. In this high-stakes profession, you already live with urgency. But God is calling you to live with eternal urgency—to see that every moment is not just fragile, but sacred.

The people you serve, the partners you work with, even the strangers you help on a call—all have eternal souls. They, like you, are a mist. Here one moment, and gone the next. The question is, what are we doing with the moments we've been given?

Eternity isn't just about what happens after death—it's about how we live today. Are we focused on things that matter? Are we walking with God, or drifting aimlessly through the sea of life? Are we using our time to build others' lives, or just trying to survive another shift?

Jesus stepped into our short "time zone" called life with an eternal purpose—to rescue you. He died and rose so that we might have peace in this life filled with purpose. When the clock is ticking and adrenaline is surging, remember, life is short, but Christ is eternal, and He invites you to live with eyes fixed on what truly lasts.

So yes—every second counts. Not just in rescue and response, but in how we respond to the One who rescued us.

Prayer

Lord, remind me that life is a mist. Help me not to waste the time I've been given but to live each moment with purpose and eternal perspective. Help me to serve with urgency, love with compassion, and trust You with every breath—and every heartbeat. May my life count for more than just survival.

Reflection Questions

1. How does the reality of life's brevity affect your
   daily decisions and outlook?

   _____

   _____

   _____

   _____

   _____

2. Are there things you've been putting off that
   God is nudging you to act on today?

   _____

   _____

   _____

   _____

   _____

3. Who in your life needs to hear the hope we have in Christ?

_____

_____

_____

_____

_____

_____

_____

_____

_____

_____

_____

_____

_____

Day 13 – The Burned-Out Soul

Truth for Today: Matthew 11:28

"Come to me, all who are weary and burdened, and I will give you rest."

There's tired—and then there's deep within the soul tired. Most first responders know the difference. You can push through physical exhaustion with caffeine and grit. But what about when your heart is heavy, your mind is frayed, and your soul feels like it's smoldering from too many fires—inside and out?

Jesus speaks directly into this. Not with guilt and shame, but with an invitation: "Come to Me." That's not a command to do more—it's a call to simply come. Less performance, less pretense, and less weight you were never meant to carry.

In a world that demands a 24/7 response, it's easy to forget that you're human. You were never designed to be everyone's savior, to absorb every tragedy, or to carry every burden without breaking. You may wear the gear of a rescuer, but you also need rescue. And Jesus offers it—not in the form of escape, but in rest for your soul.

This isn't a power nap. It's not just a day off. It's deeper than that. The kind of rest Jesus offers is deep within. It's the peace that comes from knowing you're not holding the world together—He is. It's the quiet strength of laying your weight down at the feet of the One who carried the cross.

So when the radio is quiet and the noise in your head is getting louder, remember this; rest is not a weakness—it's a must. And it's available every single day, not when the chaos ends, but in the middle of it.

Come to Me—not when you're strong and not when you've figured everything out. But when you're burned out, worn thin, and deeply weary. He's not just able to give rest—He is your rest.

Prayer

Jesus, I'm tired—not just physically, but deep down in my soul. I need Your rest. I lay down every burden I've picked up along the way. Help me to trust You more than my own strength. Be my refuge, my rest, and my renewal today.

Reflection Questions

1. What burdens have you been carrying that are draining you?

_____

_____

_____

_____

_____

2. What does it look like for you to "come to Jesus" in the middle of your fatigue?

_____

_____

_____

_____

_____

3. Do you believe rest is part of God's plan for your strength and survival?

_____

_____

_____

_____

_____

_____

_____

_____

_____

_____

_____

_____

Day 14 – Courage Isn't the Absence of Fear

Truth for Today: Joshua 1:9

"Have I not commanded you? Be strong and courageous. Do not be afraid; do not be discouraged, for the Lord your God will be with you wherever you go."

Fear isn't foreign to first responders—it's familiar.

Whether it's crawling into a burning structure, performing CPR on a lifeless body, or approaching an unknown vehicle accident at 3 a.m., you've likely felt it grip your chest and quicken your breath. The job demands courage, but not the kind the world imagines.

Courage isn't the absence of fear—it's serving in the presence of it. When God told Joshua to "be strong and courageous," He wasn't saying, "Don't ever feel fear." He was saying, "Don't be ruled by it."

Why? Because God Himself would be with him.

God-enabled courage is different from adrenaline. It doesn't come from ego or fame. It's born from trust—knowing that the same God who parted the Red Sea and crushed giants, walks with you into every call. Courage isn't something you muster up; it's something you receive when you believe that God is bigger than whatever you're facing.

You may feel afraid at times. That doesn't make you weak—it makes you human. Even Jesus, in the garden of Gethsemane, faced overwhelming sorrow and anguish before going to the cross. But He went anyway. That's courage, and through His Spirit, that same courage lives in you.

When the alarm sounds, or when your mind replays past calls, or when the future feels uncertain—remember Joshua 1:9. God has not abandoned you. He hasn't called you to courage without supplying the strength for it. Real courage doesn't ignore fear. It walks through it—with God.

Prayer

God, You know my fears—even the ones I try to hide. Thank You for being near and for calling me to be courageous—not because I'm strong, but because You're with me. Help me trust Your guidance more than I fear the unknown. Fill me with Your strength to stand, to serve, and to move forward.

Reflection Questions

1. When have you faced fear and needed to lean on God's courage instead of your own?

_____

_____

_____

_____

_____

2. Do you believe that God is with you wherever you go—on the job, in the home, in those dark places?

_____

_____

_____

_____

_____

3. What's one fear you need to move forward in faith?

_____

_____

_____

_____

_____

_____

_____

_____

_____

_____

_____

_____

_____

Day 15 – Mayday Moments

Truth for Today: Psalm 18:6

"In my distress I called to the Lord; I cried to my God for help. From his temple he heard my voice; my cry came before him, into his ears."

When a firefighter calls "Mayday," it's not casual radio communication—it's a desperate call for help. It means the situation has turned critical, the danger is overwhelming, and immediate help is needed. It's not a sign of failure, it's a call for help!

David had his own Mayday moment in Psalm 18. Surrounded by distress, overwhelmed by enemies, and shaken to the core, he did what all of us are invited to do—he cried out to the Lord. Not as a last resort, but as a first instinct. And God heard him—not from a distance, not with delay, but with divine attention, "My cry came before Him, into His ears."

Your crisis may not look like David's, but you've faced your own versions. Emotional breakdowns, traumatic calls, the weight of guilt, the fog of depression, or the shock of loss. The uniform may hide the distress, but God sees past all of it—He sees the innermost turmoil—and He hears every tear drop that falls.

Don't let pride keep you silent in your distress. Calling out isn't weakness, it's wisdom. God never ignores a mayday. When His children call, He listens. And not only does He hear, but He responds. Psalm 18 goes on to describe God rising, thundering, parting the heavens, and reaching down to pull David from deep waters.

In a similar way when Jesus died on the cross the thunder roared, the rocks split, and the graves were opened. It was heaven's rescue mission!

First responders are trained to run toward those who cry for help. How much more will the God who created you respond when you cry out?

Whatever your crisis—whether physical, mental, emotional, or spiritual—there's one name that's always worth calling. No radio required. No Mayday needed. Just a heart that says, "Lord, I need You."

Prayer

Lord, in my distress I call to You. I'm not always strong. I don't always know what to do. But I believe You hear me, even when no one else does. Reach down and steady my heart, set my feet on solid ground, and renew my mind. Rescue me from the weight I can't carry.

Reflection Questions

1. When have you experienced a personal "Mayday moment" emotionally, mentally, spiritually, or physically?

_____

_____

_____

_____

_____

2. Do you believe God hears your cries, even when you don't feel Him?

_____

_____

_____

_____

_____

3. What is one area where you need to call out to God today?

_____

_____

_____

_____

_____

_____

_____

_____

_____

_____

_____

_____

Day 16 – The Power of Partnership

Truth for Today: Ecclesiastes 4:9–10

"Two are better than one, because they have a good return for their labor: If either of them falls down, one can help the other up."

$\mathcal{I}$n the world of first responders, no one does it alone. It's always two in, two out. Whether entering a burning building, responding to a level one trauma, or working the aftermath of a tragic call, one thing is clear; you need your brothers and sisters beside you. You train together, eat together, laugh together, and sometimes cry together. That bond is powerful and unbreakable.

Ecclesiastes 4 reminds us that strength is found in partnership. One can fall alone. One can fail alone. But two? Two can lift each other up. Two can cover more ground. Two can fight longer and stand stronger. God didn't design us for isolation. He designed us for community, support, and shared burdens.

Being your brother's partner isn't just about being there in the fire, it's about being there before, during, and after the storm. It's the quiet check-in after a tough call. It's noticing when your partner's silence speaks volumes. It's the willingness to carry part of someone else's weight when they can't carry it alone.

And sometimes, you're the one who needs help. That doesn't make you weak—it makes you human. It's pride that keeps us pretending we're fine. But humility opens the door for healing. The strongest responders are the ones who know when to lean—not just when to lead.

Ultimately, there's One who never lets us fall without reaching down. Jesus didn't just check in—He came all the way down to walk with us, two in and two out. He carried our sin, and bore our burden on the cross. He proved that we don't fight alone. He is our ever-present help, our perfect Partner, and Savior. Through Him, we are never truly alone—not in the struggle, not in the fire, and not in our failures.

In the Kingdom of God, we carry one another's burdens because Christ first carried ours. We lift others up because He lifted us up from death to life. And we offer our strength to others because His strength now lives in us.

Prayer

Lord, thank You for the gift of brotherhood and support. But more than anything, thank You for Jesus—my Savior and Friend who never leaves my side. Help me lean on You in my weakness and walk with others in theirs. Give me the humility to receive help and the compassion to offer it.

Reflection Questions

1. Are you more likely to help others or hide your
    own need for help?

_____

_____

_____

_____

_____

2. Who has been a real "brother" in your life? How
    did that impact you?

_____

_____

_____

_____

_____

3. Is there someone around you who needs a quiet check-in or simple encouragement?

_____

_____

_____

_____

_____

_____

_____

_____

_____

_____

_____

_____

Day 17 – Behind the Mask

Truth for Today: 1 Samuel 16:7

"The Lord does not look at the things people look at. People look at the outward appearance, but the Lord looks at the heart."

$\mathcal{E}$very shift, you put on a mask—sometimes literally, sometimes emotionally. Whether it's a helmet, SCBA, or simply a hardened face, first responders get good at hiding what's really going on inside. You show up strong, composed, and steady. That's what everyone expects. That's what your team needs. But what about the part of you no one sees?

When Samuel went to anoint Israel's next king, he assumed the biggest and strongest son would be the obvious choice. But God stopped him and reminded him, "Man looks at the outward appearance, but I look at the heart." God doesn't need your armor. He doesn't need your mask. He's not impressed by your performance or fooled by your words. He knows the real you—and loves you anyway.

You don't have to pretend to be strong with God. In fact, He does His best work when we admit our weakness. Vulnerability isn't a liability; it's the starting place of humility and healing. When you remove the mask before

God, you won't find judgment but grace—not rejection but restoration.

That's what the gospel is all about. Jesus didn't come for the strong, but for the weak. He took on flesh to rescue the real you—the one behind the uniform, behind the badge, behind the mask. On the cross, He bore every hidden wound, carried every silent struggle, and took on every sin we try to hide. In His resurrection, He offers us a new identity—a new life.

You're not just a first responder—you're a son or daughter of the King. And He's not looking at your rank, your reputation, or your résumé. He's looking at your heart.

Prayer

Father, I admit that I often hide behind strength, silence, or routine. But You see my heart—and You don't turn away. Thank You for sending Jesus to meet me behind the mask, to carry my burdens, and to love me as I truly am. Help me live openly before You, receiving grace where I've hidden shame. And give me the courage to let others in, just as You let me in.

Reflection Questions

1. What emotional or spiritual masks do you tend to wear, even with God?

_____

_____

_____

_____

2. How does it feel to know God sees you fully and still chooses you?

_____

_____

_____

_____

3. What would it look like to let someone else see the real you today?

_____

_____

_____

_____

_____

_____

_____

_____

_____

_____

_____

Day 18 – Prepared for the Unknown

Truth for Today: Proverbs 3:5–6

"Trust in the Lord with all your heart and lean not on your own understanding; in all your ways submit to him, and he will make your paths straight."

---

*E*very call brings uncertainty. You gear up, get the address, and head out, but you don't really know what you're walking into. Smoke conditions change. Scenes escalate. Patients crash. What started as routine can turn sideways in seconds. So you prepare for the unknown because it's what you signed up for.

But how do you prepare internally? How do you stay steady when everything around you is shifting?

Proverbs 3:5–6 isn't a verse about avoiding danger. It's a call to trust God when the outcome isn't clear. He doesn't promise that you'll always understand what's happening. In fact, He tells you not to lean on your own understanding. Instead, He calls you to trust Him with all your heart—especially when the road ahead disappears.

You don't have to know everything. You don't have to see the whole scene. Faith doesn't mean you ignore the danger. It means you step forward with confidence that God goes before you.

Jesus "trusted in the Lord" with "all His heart" even as His blood was being poured out like a drink offering on the cross. He didn't lean on His own understanding, but trusted His Father all the way—at the cost of His life. Through every trial, He leaned on the One who sent Him and never wavered in faith. In every way, Jesus submitted to His Father, obedient to the point of death—even death on a cross (Philippians 2:8).

The same God who raised Jesus from the dead is fully capable of guiding your path, on the job, in your relationships, and in your decisions. You may not know what's coming next, but He does—and He's already gone before you to help.

You bring your training. You bring your gear. But more than anything, bring your trust. Because when your understanding fails—and it will—His faithfulness never does.

Prayer

Lord, I don't always know what's ahead. I face unknowns at work and in life that stretch me beyond my understanding. But today I choose to trust You. Lead me where I can't see. Guide me when I don't understand. And give me the peace that comes from knowing You're already there with me.

Reflection Questions

1. What current situations in your life feel uncertain or unclear?

_____

_____

_____

_____

2. Are there areas where you've been leaning more on your own understanding than God's wisdom?

_____

_____

_____

_____

3. What would it look like today to trust God with all your heart?

_____

_____

_____

_____

_____

_____

_____

_____

_____

_____

_____

_____

_____

Day 19 – The Debrief

Truth for Today: Lamentations 3:23

"They are new every morning; great is your faithfulness."

---

*A*fter a hard call or a tough shift, there's the debrief. It's the moment when you step back, review what happened, and try to make sense of it all. What went right, what didn't, and what still lingers in your mind. But not everything can be solved in a few minutes around a table. Some wounds go deeper. Some images stick.

That's where grace steps in.

Lamentations was written in a time of deep sorrow and devastation. The author was surrounded by loss and ruin, yet right in the middle of that pain, he clings to this unshakable truth, "His mercies are new every morning." That means no matter what yesterday held, failure, regret, or grief—God offers a fresh start, every day.

You might carry guilt over a call that didn't go the way you hoped. Maybe you lost your cool. Maybe you froze. Maybe you just feel emotionally and mentally drained. But the debrief isn't just about what you did—it's also about what God has done for you.

This is the heart of the gospel—Jesus stepped into our place, carried our burdens, and bore our guilt, so we wouldn't have to carry it all. He took the weight of sin, shame, and sorrow on Himself at the cross. And because of His sacrifice, you are not defined by your worst moments, but by His perfect performance. You don't have to earn a second chance—He's already secured it through His blood.

So when you sit there with your pain, your questions, or regrets, remember; His mercy is new every morning—through blood-bought grace. Grace that covers every failure. Grace that heals every wound. Grace that walks with you through every shift, every sorrow, and every struggle.

Let the debrief be more than just a checklist. Let it be a sacred moment of reflection. Lay your day before God. Thank Him for His mercy. Trust in the finished work of Christ. And wake up tomorrow knowing a new day has come.

Prayer

Father, thank You for fresh mercy, purchased for me through the cross. Some days leave me tired, confused, or heavy-hearted—but You offer new grace, not because I've earned it, but because Jesus paid the price. Help me process what I've seen, heard, and done with honesty—and help me receive Your love and forgiveness.

Reflection Questions

1. What recent experience are you still trying to
    process or debrief internally?

_____

_____

_____

_____

_____

2. How does it feel to know God's mercy meets
    you there—new every morning?

_____

_____

_____

_____

_____

3. What would it look like to receive God's grace for
    yourself today?

_____

_____

_____

_____

_____

_____

_____

_____

_____

_____

_____

_____

Day 20 – Shield of Faith

Truth for Today: Ephesians 6:16

"In addition to all this, take up the shield of faith, with which you can extinguish all the flaming arrows of the evil one."

---

*Y*our shield is your lifeline. Every first responder knows the importance of carrying the right gear. Without it, you're exposed, vulnerable, and when the heat turns up—you don't have time to go looking for your gear. It has to be on you, and ready for battle.

In Ephesians 6, Paul tells believers to "take up the shield of faith." Why? Because there are flaming arrows being fired at your heart and mind, accusations, temptations, fears, doubts, and lies. You may not see them coming, but you'll feel their impact if you're unprotected.

Faith is your shield. It's not blind belief or wishful thinking—it's trusting God's character when life gets chaotic. It's choosing to believe His Word over what fear whispers. It's lifting your eyes above the flames and fixing them on the One who is going through it with you.

The enemy wants to wear you down with discouragement. He wants to convince you that you're alone, that you're not enough, or that God isn't coming through. But when you raise your shield, those arrows don't stand a chance.

Remember, Jesus' body was our shield. He protected us from God's judgment—extinguishing the flames that were meant for us. He bore our punishment and pain—and we escaped without a scratch. His flesh was torn so we could be healed. His life was taken so we could live.

In Roman times, soldiers would link their shields together, side by side, forming a wall of protection. That's what we do in faith with our brothers and sisters—stand shield to shield, covering and protecting each other.

So today, lift your shield of faith, and trust God to protect what you can't. Stand firm in who He is, even when you can't make sense of what's happening around you. You're not unarmed or uncovered. You carry the shield of faith—and it extinguishes the flames.

Prayer

Lord, I lift my shield of faith today. I trust You to protect me—body, mind, and soul. When fear attacks, remind me of Your promises. When lies come, let truth be my defense. Help me stand with others in faith, not retreat in isolation. Thank You for being my shield and my strength.

Reflection Questions

1. What "flaming arrows" have you been facing lately—doubt, fear, lies, temptation?

_____

_____

_____

_____

2. What does it look like to take up your shield of faith today, practically?

_____

_____

_____

_____

3. Are you linking shields with others, or trying to stand alone?

_____

_____

_____

_____

_____

_____

_____

_____

_____

_____

_____

_____

Day 21 – Through Smoke and Soot

Truth for Today: Job 23:10

"But he knows the way that I take; when he has tested me, I will come forth as gold."

The fire burns hot and the smoke is thick. The scene is traumatic, and soot clings to everything. Whether you're on the fire or simply walking through a season of personal struggle, the truth remains, some of life's greatest tests come through the flames.

Job knew this kind of fire. He didn't face burning buildings, but he did face deep, relentless suffering, loss, confusion, and silence from heaven. And yet, in the middle of the ashes, Job clung to a stunning truth—God knows the way I take. Even when Job didn't understand what was happening, he believed that his pain had purpose, and that he wouldn't be lost in the fire.

And neither will you.

This is more than positive thinking. It's the promise of the gospel. You see, the ultimate suffering was borne by Jesus Christ, who entered suffering in your place. He wasn't just tested; He was crushed, so that you could be refined. Because He rose from the grave, suffering will never be the end of your story.

God does not waste the pain of His people. Every hardship, every fire, every question is allowed by a Father who loves you too much to leave you as you are. He is shaping you. Refining you. Purifying your faith so that Christ shines more clearly through your life.

Sometimes, the smoke makes it hard to see. Sometimes the pain makes it hard to breathe. But the truth remains; if you belong to Jesus, the fire cannot destroy you—it can only refine you. Your identity is not in the trauma you've experienced or the ashes you carry; it's in the blood of Christ that cleanses you.

And when the flames die down and the smoke clears, you'll still be standing, not because you're strong, but because He is faithful.

Prayer

Jesus, thank You for entering the fire for me, bearing the judgment I deserved and rising again to give me hope. In my own suffering, remind me that You suffered greater still. You are with me, working through it and refining me. Strengthen my trust when I can't see clearly, and remind me that I'll come forth victorious, because You already won the victory.

Reflection Questions

1. What "fires" or tests are you walking through right now?

_____

_____

_____

_____

_____

2. How does the gospel help you endure suffering with hope?

_____

_____

_____

_____

_____

3. Can you see the ways God is refining your faith through hardship?

_____

_____

_____

_____

_____

_____

_____

_____

_____

_____

_____

_____

Day 22 – Not Alone in the Fire

Truth for Today: Daniel 3:25

"Look! I see four men walking around in the fire, unbound and unharmed, and the fourth looks like a son of the gods."

The fire was real. The furnace was heated seven times hotter than normal. Shadrach, Meshach, and Abednego didn't escape the flames—they were thrown in. But when the King looked inside, he didn't see three burning men. He saw four.

And that fourth figure changed everything.

God never promised to keep His people out of the fire, but He did promise to be with them in it. That's what makes the difference for you too. As a first responder, you face real fires—sometimes mental, physical, emotional, or spiritual. There are moments when you feel the heat, when the pressure is intense, and when your strength is pushed to the edge.

The gospel tells us that Jesus didn't stay at a distance—He stepped into the fire with us, came to earth, took on flesh, and walked through suffering, rejection, and death, so we would never have to walk in the fire without Him by our side.

Jesus was bound and harmed on the cross as He endured the furnace of God's punishment for our sin. He took what we deserved so we could walk away from the flames, unbound and unharmed. Unbound from our slavery to sin (or addiction) and unharmed from its consuming fire.

When life burns around you, when trials close in, and when the air gets filled with thick black smoke, look again—there's another in the fire with you.

You may not always feel or see Him, but He's there. You may not understand why the fire came, but the cross proves His love for you. You may walk through flames, but in Christ, you are never walking alone.

Your uniform may carry the smoke of yesterday's battle. Your soul may still ache from past calls. But you are not forsaken. You are protected and loved by the One who walks with you, and brings you out from the furnace, unbound and unharmed.

Prayer

Jesus, thank You that You don't watch from a distance—you walk through the fire with me. When life burns hot and I feel overwhelmed, remind me of Your presence. Strengthen my heart with the truth that You've already faced the ultimate fire at the cross—and You did it for me.

Reflection Questions

1. What "fires" are you currently walking through?

_____

_____

_____

_____

2. How does the presence of Christ change how you face trials?

_____

_____

_____

_____

_____

3. When have you seen evidence that you were not alone in the fire?

_____

_____

_____

_____

_____

_____

_____

_____

_____

_____

_____

_____

_____

Day 23 – When You Can't Save Everyone

Truth for Today: Romans 12:15

"Rejoice with those who rejoice; mourn with those who mourn."

$\mathcal{Y}$ou train to save lives. You respond to the worst moments of someone's life with skill, speed, and strength. And still… sometimes it's not enough.

There are calls that end with silence. Scenes that keep playing through your mind. Names you remember. Faces you can't forget. And though you did everything you could, the weight remains, because you couldn't save them all. This is the part they don't teach in the academy, how to carry the grief that lingers when your head finally hits the pillow.

Romans 12:15 calls us not to move past pain quickly but to enter into it with compassion: "Mourn with those who mourn." That includes others, and that includes yourself.

But the gospel offers something deeper than emotional relief—it offers redemptive hope. Jesus didn't just mourn death, He conquered it. At the tomb of Lazarus, He wept (John 11:35). Fully God, fully man, yet still moved by grief. And then He called the dead to life.

On the cross, Jesus bore not only sin, but also the full weight of human suffering, including yours. His resurrection wasn't just a miracle, it was a declaration that death doesn't have the final word.

You may not be able to save everyone, but Jesus came to save anyone who believes in Him. That truth doesn't erase grief, but it does redeem it. It reminds you that your efforts are not in vain, even when the outcome hurts. You reflect the heart of God when you show up, give your all, and weep for the ones you couldn't rescue.

God doesn't expect you to carry the weight of every loss. He invites you to lay that weight at the foot of the cross, where the Man of Sorrows bore grief beyond measure—and rose to give peace that surpasses understanding.

So let yourself mourn.
But don't mourn alone.
And never mourn without hope.

Prayer

Jesus, You know what it means to mourn. You wept at the tomb, and You weep with me now. I give You the sorrow I carry, and the weight of the ones I couldn't save. Help me not to run from grief but to bring it to You. Thank You that because of the cross, death is not the end, and because of the resurrection, hope is still alive.

Reflection Questions

1. Are you carrying grief from someone you couldn't save or a scene you can't forget?

_____

_____

_____

_____

2. How does knowing that Jesus mourned, and rose from the grave, bring you comfort?

_____

_____

_____

_____

3. What would it look like to lay your sorrow at the feet of Christ today?

_____

_____

_____

_____

_____

_____

_____

_____

_____

_____

_____

_____

_____

Day 24 – Firehouse Family

Truth for Today: Galatians 6:2

"Carry each other's burdens, and in this way you will fulfill the law of Christ."

$\mathcal{T}$here's something sacred about the firehouse and shift crew. It's more than just a group of coworkers, it's a family. You eat together, laugh together, argue like siblings, and respond to chaos of all kinds side by side. In the heat of a call or the quiet moments in between, bonds are built that few others understand.

But even in that close-knit community, burdens often stay hidden. Everyone wants to look strong, hold it together, carry their own weight. Yet Galatians 6:2 tells us to; "Carry each other's burdens, and in this way you will fulfill the law of Christ."

What is the law of Christ? It's love. Sacrificial and shoulder-to-shoulder—just like Jesus. The kind Jesus showed when He carried your burden, not just emotional weight, but the crushing weight of sin. He took it all on Himself, not because you deserved it, but because He couldn't bear to leave you buried under it.

That's the gospel—Christ carrying what we couldn't. And now, because you've been lifted by His grace, you're called to extend that grace to others. Not with easy answers or shallow encouragement, but with compassion, and a willingness to step into someone else's burdens.

This is what the firehouse family is meant to be. A place where real strength is found in honesty. A crew that not only runs into danger together, but also leans on each other when the job becomes too heavy to carry alone.

So carry each other's burdens the way you'd carry someone from a burning building, remembering that Jesus carried the weight of the world and fulfilled the law of love.

Prayer

Jesus, thank You for carrying my greatest burden at the cross. You didn't leave me to suffer alone, and I don't want to leave others alone either. Help me love my brothers and sisters with the same compassion You showed me. Make our crew more than a team, make us a reflection of Your love.

Reflection Questions

1. Are you carrying a burden that someone else could help lift?

_____

_____

_____

_____

_____

2. Who around you might be silently struggling and needs someone to come alongside them?

_____

_____

_____

_____

_____

3. How does the gospel reshape how you view strength, community, and vulnerability?

_____

_____

_____

_____

_____

_____

_____

_____

_____

_____

_____

_____

_____

Day 25 – Training Day

Truth for Today: 1 Timothy 4:7

"Train yourself to be godly."

---

*B*efore you ever put on the uniform, you trained. You ran drills, studied manuals, lifted weights, practiced procedures, and pushed your body and mind to their limits, because lives would one day depend on it. You train to be ready, alert, and sharp in the moment when it matters most.

Paul told Timothy, "Train yourself to be godly." Just like physical training requires consistency, sweat, and sacrifice, so does spiritual growth. Godliness doesn't just happen because you show up to work or even because you've believed in Jesus—it grows when you discipline your life around the gospel.

But here's the key, training doesn't earn God's approval, Christ already accomplished that for you. The gospel tells us that salvation is a gift, not a reward. You don't train to become accepted, you train because you already are. You train because God's grace is so good. You train because you've been rescued, and you want to live like someone who's free.

So how do you train? You live knowing that He is with you and will never leave you. You stay connected to other believers. You talk to Him through pain instead of trying to numb it. You confess your weaknesses instead of hiding them. You rehearse the truth of the gospel until it becomes your first reflex, not your last resort.

And just like physical training, there will be days it feels like progress is slow. But remember, learning and growing comes over time, not overnight. God is patient, and His Spirit is in you, strengthening your faith, shaping your character, and preparing you to stand strong.

On the job, your training may save lives on earth. In your walk with Christ, your training could impact lives for eternity. So don't neglect your training, train like someone who knows the victory is already won.

Prayer

Father, thank You that my salvation doesn't depend on how well I perform, but on what Jesus already finished. Help me grow, not out of guilt, but out of love. Give me the discipline to train my heart around Your truth, and make me strong in spirit to serve.

Reflection Questions

1. How patient are you being with yourself as you learn and grow in Christ?

_____

_____

_____

_____

_____

2. In what ways could you be more disciplined, not to earn God's grace, but because you've already received it?

_____

_____

_____

_____

_____

3. What can you do today to strengthen your walk with Christ?

_____

_____

_____

_____

_____

_____

_____

_____

_____

_____

_____

_____

_____

Day 26 – The Still Small Voice

Truth for Today: 1 Kings 19:12

"After the fire came a gentle whisper…"

---

*A*s a first responder, you're trained to react to the commotion. Sirens, screams, alarms—the sounds of crisis. You're constantly on alert, tuned into trouble, trained to take control when everything else is out of control.

But what happens when the call is over, and silence falls? What do you do when the adrenaline fades and you're left alone with your thoughts? Where do you turn when your soul feels scorched by all you've seen—and God is silent? That's where Elijah found himself.

Elijah had just faced down evil in a miraculous showdown at Mount Carmel. Fire from heaven. A victory everyone saw. Yet shortly after, he was burned out, afraid, and hiding in a cave. God told him to stand on the mountain. A powerful wind tore through. Then an earthquake. Then fire. But God wasn't in any of it. He was in the whisper. The whisper wasn't just His voice—it was His presence drawing near.

God doesn't shout to compete with your thoughts. He waits for it to quiet. And then, in the stillness, He speaks. As a firefighter, EMT, or medic, you may be more comfortable running into danger than sitting in silence. But it's in those quiet moments—when you stop performing and start listening—that God speaks most clearly.

You may not hear an audible voice, but the Spirit of God speaks through His Word, through prayer, through worship, and even in your conscience. Here's the truth; God doesn't just meet you in the chaos—He meets you in the silence. He doesn't wait for you to be perfect, polished, or put together.

He draws near to the broken-hearted, the discouraged, and the ones ready to give up. Jesus didn't come with fanfare. He came in a manger. He didn't crush His enemies with thunder. He conquered death with a cross. And even now, He speaks, not just in the storm, but in the stillness.

The next time everything goes quiet, don't rush to fill the silence. Pause. Listen. He may be whispering to your heart just how loved you are.

Prayer

Lord, with the uproar of this world and the noise of my work, it's easy to miss Your voice. Help me slow down. Quiet my soul. Train my ears to hear Your still small voice. Thank You for meeting me not only in the action, but in the stillness.

Reflection Questions

1. When was the last time you sat in silence and listened for God?

_____

_____

_____

_____

_____

2. Do you expect Him to speak in big, dramatic ways—or are you willing to meet Him in the quiet?

_____

_____

_____

_____

_____

3. How can you create an environment today to hear His still small voice?

_____

_____

_____

_____

_____

_____

_____

_____

_____

_____

_____

_____

Day 27 – When the Smoke Clears

Truth for Today: Revelation 21:4

"He will wipe every tear from their eyes. There will be no more death or mourning or crying or pain, for the old order of things has passed away."

---

*A*fter the call ends, after the smoke settles, after the gear comes off, what's left? The smell lingers. The memories stick. Some calls you carry for life. You may be able to clean your uniform, but you can't always clear your mind.

The pain isn't just physical—it's emotional, mental, and spiritual too. Some wounds can't be stitched. Some memories can't be unseen. And sometimes, the weight of it all feels heavier than your turnout gear ever was.

But God promises something the job never could, a day when the smoke will finally clear, and healing will be complete. Revelation 21:4 is not a wish. It's a guarantee. A real moment in the future when God Himself will personally wipe away every tear. No more trauma. No more mourning. No more death.

This isn't the end of your story. This is the beginning of what you were made for. That's the promise of the gospel. Because of Jesus, who entered our broken world, bore our sin, and conquered death, you are not heading toward destruction, you are headed for restoration.

Not temporary relief, but eternal renewal. Not just a moment of peace, but a home of healing. That's what gives meaning to the mess. That's what gives purpose to the pain. You don't serve in vain, you don't suffer unseen.

You are running toward a place where the alarm will never sound again, and the tears will never fall again, because Jesus will make all things new.

So if today still feels too heavy to carry, if you're choking on the smoke of grief or regret, if you're asking how much more your heart can hold, look up and look ahead, because the day is coming when there will be no more death, no more mourning, no more tears, and no more pain.

Prayer

Lord, some things I've seen are hard to carry. Some wounds don't seem to heal. But I believe Your promise, that one day, You'll wipe away every tear. Thank You Jesus, for giving me hope beyond the fire. Until that day, help me hold to Your truth and press forward in faith.

Reflection Questions

1. What part of the job has left lasting wounds in your heart?

_____

_____

_____

_____

2. How does the promise of "no more tears" encourage you in your grief or trauma?

_____

_____

_____

_____

3. How can you live with an eternal view, even when the smoke hasn't cleared yet?

_____

_____

_____

_____

_____

_____

_____

_____

_____

_____

_____

_____

_____

_____

Day 28 – A Higher Command

Truth for Today: Colossians 3:23–24

"Whatever you do, work at it with all your heart, as working for the Lord, not for human masters… It is the Lord Christ you are serving."

---

*E*very first responder knows the importance of the chain of command. Orders, roles, and authority matter. You train to act without hesitation, because lives are on the line. But sometimes the people you serve don't appreciate you.

Sometimes the public misunderstands you. Sometimes the recognition never comes, the sacrifice isn't seen, and the thanks never shows up. That's when you remember, you serve under a higher command.

Paul wrote to everyday believers—people working hard, often without applause—and told them what really mattered; "Work as for the Lord."

Not for supervisors. Not for approval. Not for recognition, but for Christ. That changes everything. When you put on the uniform, you're not just representing your agency, you're carrying the name of Jesus into each place, chaotic scenes, and broken lives.

Whether you're pulling hose, running a trauma scene, sitting in the ambulance, or cleaning up after a hard shift, you're working under a different command system. And God sees everything—your effort, your patience, your endurance, and your heart.

Even when others overlook it, Christ doesn't. And even when no one else rewards you, He will. Paul says that from the Lord *"you will receive the inheritance as your reward."* You're not just clocking hours, you're investing in eternity.

That doesn't mean every shift will run with perfection. It means that even in the most routine calls, you have a higher purpose. Not just to serve the city… but to serve the King. Jesus didn't just serve us by dying, He served us by living in obedience to the Father.

He humbled Himself, took the lowest position by becoming a servant, was misunderstood, mistreated, and killed, but ultimately exalted. Now He invites you to serve in the same spirit, not to earn His favor, but because you already have it.

Prayer

Jesus, thank You for calling me to serve, and for reminding me that I ultimately serve You. Help me to work with excellence, integrity, and humility. When I'm tired or overlooked, remind me that You see. Let every shift be an offering to You.

Reflection Questions

1. Who are you really working for, people's approval or God's?

_____

_____

_____

_____

_____

2. How would your mindset change if you started every shift "for the Lord"?

_____

_____

_____

_____

_____

3. What does it mean to serve with honor, even when no one sees or cares?

_____

_____

_____

_____

_____

_____

_____

_____

_____

_____

_____

_____

Day 29 – A Powerful Light

Truth for Today: Matthew 5:14

"You are the light of the world. A city set on a hill cannot be hidden."

---

*Y*ou may not feel like it, but you carry real candle power—not the kind that comes with a badge or a title, the kind that comes from God. Jesus said, "You are the light of the world." That means even one person who shines can expel the darkness.

On the job, in the firehouse, in the ambulance, or on the street. One moment of compassion, one act of love. One quiet prayer when no one else is praying. You may not be able to fix everything or reach everyone—but you can shine right where you are.

The world you work in is dark. You see addiction, abuse, trauma, death, and despair all on a daily basis. But the light of Christ wasn't made to shine only in safe places. It was made for the dark, and it just needs to be present.

A single candle can illuminate a whole room. A single firefighter or medic, who walks in love, truth, and grace can shine with eternal impact. So don't underestimate your influence.

Your quiet faithfulness matters. Your Christ-like character leaves a mark. Your willingness to stand apart, even when it costs something, speaks louder than words ever could. And there's the gospel at the center of it all. Jesus is the source of the light.

The Light of the World (John 8:12) entered the darkness for you—absorbing it on the cross and overcoming it with His blood. And when He lives in you, His light turns even your darkest places into reflections of His power, presence, and love.

Let that truth empower you today. You don't need a crowd to change the culture. You don't need a stage to make a difference. Be an influence. Make a difference. Lead with integrity.

Prayer

Lord, sometimes I feel small and surrounded by darkness. But You said I am the light of the world, not because of who I am, but because of who You are in me. Help me help someone today. Help me live with courage, integrity, and compassion. And use my life to make a difference.

Reflection Questions

1. Where has God placed you to impact others right now?

_____

_____

_____

_____

2. How can one small act of Christ-like character make a difference for the crew?

_____

_____

_____

_____

3. Are you willing to be the one, when no one else is?

_____

_____

_____

_____

_____

_____

_____

_____

_____

_____

_____

_____

Day 30 – The Last Call

Truth for Today: 2 Timothy 4:7

"I have fought the good fight, I have finished the race, I have kept the faith."

One day, all the calls will stop. The gear will be retired, the tones will go silent, the work of your hands will be done. But the legacy of how you lived—and who you served—will live on.

In his final letter, the apostle Paul looked back at a life of service, not one without hardship, but one filled with purpose.

- He didn't say, "I won every battle."
- He said, "I fought the good fight."
- He didn't boast about perfection.
- He rejoiced in faithfulness.

That's your call too. You may not feel like a hero. You've no doubt made mistakes along the way. But if you keep showing up, keep serving, keep striving, you'll finish well. This journey of being a first responder is more than just a job. It's a mission.

And if you do it with integrity, faith, and love, it becomes a legacy people remember;

- How you led.
- How you cared.
- How you spoke.
- How you stood for what was right.

And most of all, how you finished the call with honor. But there's something even greater—something far beyond our own service:

Jesus said, 'It is finished,' as He hung on that dreadful, dark, and lonely cross. Though nailed there like a criminal and mocked as a counterfeit, one of the soldiers nearby, seeing how He died, said, 'Surely this was the Son of God.'"

Jesus finished His last call and gave all that He had—His life, His breath, His spirit. And one day He will remember your faith in Him and say, "Well done, good and faithful servant," not because you were flawless, but because you were His child.

You don't have to earn your worth, Jesus already secured it for you. You don't have to finish in your own strength, He finished it for you, and gave you His Spirit who empowers you. You don't have to fear the end, because eternal life has already begun.

So finish strong, not just your shift or your career, but finish the call of life with eternity in view. Let that be your legacy—faithful, courageous, redeemed, and loved.

Prayer

Jesus, thank You for walking with me through every call, every shift, every season. Help me to finish well, not just in my work, but in my life. Let my legacy reflect Your faithfulness. Strengthen me to keep the faith, to fight the good fight, and to finish the race with honor.

Reflection Questions

1. What do you want those you've served with to remember about your life?

_____

_____

_____

_____

2. What does it mean for you to finish well, not just as a responder, but as a follower of Christ?

_____

_____

_____

_____

3. Where is God calling you to keep fighting the good
    fight today?

_____

_____

_____

_____

_____

_____

_____

_____

_____

_____

_____

_____

Afterword – Standing Firm in the Fire

This 30-day journey was never about surviving the flames—it's about standing firm in the fire through faith in Christ. Every truth you've read reminds you that you are not alone in the battle. The same God who called you to serve is the One who stands with you in every trial, every call, and every moment.

Your faith has been tested, but it is being refined—made stronger, purer, and more unshakable. The fire that once threatened to destroy you is now the very place where Christ reveals His power and presence in you. He is your strength when you're weary, your peace in the chaos, and your shield in the fight.

Keep your eyes fixed on Jesus when the alarms sound and the world around you crumbles. Remember that courage comes from within—and it flows from Christ who lives in you. You don't endure by willpower but by His power working in and through you.

May your life shine like a light through the smoke and in the darkness of this world. And may your faith, tested by fire, prove genuine to the glory of God.

Other Books by Erick Hurt

Coming Soon

- **This is Real Love:** A 30-Day Devotional on True Love

- **Is This the End?:** A 30-Day Devotional for Those Losing or Lost Loved Ones

- **Be Sober Minded:** A 30-Day Devotional on Transforming Your Mind

- **No Condemnation:** A 30-Day Devotional for Those Who Have Served Time

For more updates, visit ErickHurt.com.

Invitation

If this devotional has encouraged you, I'd love to hear from you. How is God working in your life? How has this devotional blessed you? How can I pray for you or serve you?

Your story matters. Your testimony of God's grace could be the encouragement someone else needs to keep going. Feel free to share your thoughts, prayer requests, or what God is doing in your life—I'd be honored to listen, pray, and celebrate with you.

Group Leader's Guide: Faith Under Fire

Purpose of the Group

To anchor First Responders in the truth of the gospel, renew their identity in Christ, and help them walk in daily gospel freedom—together.

How to Use This Devotional in a Group

1. Weekly Gatherings (Recommended)
- Meet once a week to discuss the 7 devotionals from that week.

- Choose a quiet space where everyone can share comfortably.

2. Everyone Reads Daily
- Group members read one devotional each day (30 days total).

- Encourage members to write in their books—prayers, notes, and reflections.

3. Focus on Jesus
- Each session is centered on the finished work of Christ.

- Help participants see how every lesson points to Him—His death, resurrection, and their new life in Him.

Suggested Weekly Group Format (60–75 minutes)

1. Welcome & Prayer (5 minutes)
Begin with a warm welcome and a short prayer. Ask God to guide your time together.

2. Check-In (10–15 minutes)
Ask each person to share briefly how the week went and how the devotionals impacted them.
Example question: "What truth encouraged or challenged you this week?"

3. Scripture Focus (10 minutes)
Choose one or two key Scriptures from the past week's devotionals. Read them aloud together and ask what stood out or how they point to Christ.

4. Group Discussion (25–30 minutes)
Use the core discussion questions below to guide conversation. Encourage honesty, listening, and gospel-centered sharing.

5. Application & Prayer (15 minutes)
Close by asking: "How can we pray for you?" Spend time praying for one another, focusing on gospel hope, freedom, and transformation.

Core Discussion Questions (repeat weekly)

1. **What truth stood out most to you this week?**

2. **Where did you feel challenged, or encouraged?**

3. **How did the gospel become more real to you?**

4. **What is God inviting you to give up or believe?**

5. **How can we pray for you this week?**

Leader Encouragement

You and I are not the experts—Jesus is. Be a good listener, quick to listen and slow to speak. Try not to be a fixer. Stay focused on the gospel, not behavior change. The goal is heart transformation through the finished work of Christ.

www.ingramcontent.com/pod-product-compliance
Lightning Source LLC
Chambersburg PA
CBHW060621130626
46555CB00002B/598